you glad
you like my book ———.
You are one of my favorite
Aunts and I hope to see
you over the holidays !
Merry Christmas
'Butch'
12/88

DELAWARE... Close to home

DELAWARE... Close to home

by
FRED COMEGYS

Foreword by
AL CARTWRIGHT

THE JARED COMPANY, PUBLISHERS, WILMINGTON, DELAWARE

Special thanks to The News-Journal Company

Photographs:	Fred Comegys
Foreword:	Al Cartwright
Picture Editor:	Pat Crowe
Cover Design:	Ben Pearce
Publisher:	Alisa Dadone
Editor:	Rebecca Reed & Mary L. Allen
Project Coordinators:	Beverly & Ted Paul
Rear Jacket Photo:	Butch Comegys

THE JARED COMPANY
833 Locust Street
P. O. Box 1948
Wilmington, Delaware 19899

Published 1988
Printed and Bound in Hong Kong
Library of Congress Catalog Card Number 88-8177
ISBN: 0-89802-520-6

First Edition: November, 1988

CONTENTS

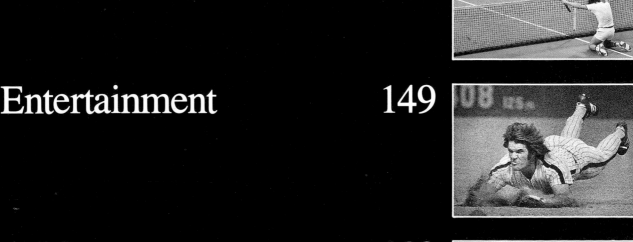

DEDICATION

This book is dedicated to my mother and my children, Butch and Candace.

ACKNOWLEDGEMENTS

I would like to thank: Pat Crowe for his immense help in laying out the book and being a friend through all our years at the News-Journal. Al Cartwright, again as a friend and for an excellent foreword. Donaghey Brown for his patience over the years. J.D. Brandt and the News-Journal. Bob Walker and Sam Buccio who in their own way, got me started at the News-Journal. Maxim Dadoun, who through his persistance, made me get the book done. To my wife Terry. Mike Biggs for suggesting the book to Max.

To all of my brothers and sisters whom I dearly love and especially my brother Terry for his strength.

And last but not least, to all the people of my home state of Delaware who have allowed me to photograph them.

Thank you,
Fred Comegys

FOREWORD
By Al Cartwright

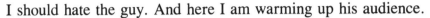

I should hate the guy. And here I am warming up his audience.

Fred Comegys...all that talent. All that hair, too.

This is coming from a frustrated photographer.

Comegys makes his living and his reputation and his prizes taking pictures for a newspaper.

Comegys on high

I made my living writing stories and columns for newspapers, all the while closet-wishing I could be making it with a camera instead of a quill, a typewriter and a word processor, in that sequence. If only I knew more about *f* stops than shortstops, I would muse, laconically, I could combine that technical jazz with my brilliant ability to read the makings of a good picture and I would be the next Margaret Bourke-White.

So, resignedly, I got my kicks taking ofttimes fuzzy family/vacation shots and, when I was sports editor and laying out the pages, playing the hell out of any good shots that came my way—usually 20 seconds before deadline; sometimes you had to wring them out—from the plumbing of the photo department.

But, enough of the eat-your-heart-out stuff.

Being in the same book with Fred Comegys is close enough to fulfillment. Start turning these pages and you won't need me, nor national judges, to inform you that this slightly overfed and athletic 46-year-old teddy bear is a grand master of newspaper photography. Dinosaur that I am, I refuse to refer to his field as ''photojournalism'', which is a grating new word in the trade.

Photojournalism makes it sound as if its practitioners make their rounds in phaetons—or possibly on howdahs—tripods and smoking jackets at the ready, virtually poised to take pictures of a subject on a date set up a fortnight ago. Or even two weeks ago. And to continue the image, their best shots would appear in the rotogravure section another fortnight hence.

Fred Comegys is a photojournalist the way Bob Leary and Ralph Moyed, his contemporaries in his neighboring news room, are journalists. They are

Comegys and Big Nose

Newspaper Guys. You can tell it by the way they work and what comes out of their work. They have a lot in common as no-frills champions of their trade. Why, all three even retain the same tailor.

This major-league picture book that is in your hands was somebody's idea because of all the laurels that have come Comegys' way, and it is about time it materialized. You must know by now that he was the Newspaper Photographer of the Year in 1985 *Nationally,* that is. His portfolio was selected #1 by the Missouri School of Journalism, the National Press Photographers Association and Canon U.S.A. There were 1,500 entrants.

Just being picked Newspaper Photographer of the Year on the News-Journal staff, if there were such an honor, would have been quite a bauble in itself. A stablemate, Pat Crowe, is a past winner of the national prize (a Lensie?). Chuck McGowen is a past runner-up. The staff has turned out such as Bill Snead, Fred's first boss, now of the Washington Post; Gary Settle, who was drafted by the New York Times, and Kevin Fleming and Jodi Cobb of National Geographic. Great photography is synonymous with the Wilmington papers. When one of the News-Journal camerapersons wins a competition, people yawn.

Thus, the national judges didn't discover Fred Comegys. He has had awards coming out of his ears for years.

My hirsute friend has done it his way. Much has been made of his starting in the newspaper business as an aimless just-out-of-high-school News-Journal copy boy in 1959. Could have been. I was there at the time, doing hard time, but I can't place him in that role, Maybe it's because we also had copy girls. I believe I first took notice of him after he had taken his first step up—or sideways—working in the photo-engraving department when pictures were etched upon zinc.

Anyhow, biographically speaking, he eventually sidled into the photo department with the title of laboratory assistant (let's face it—he was a dark-room guy) with no previous experience in that field. And from there, he bought his first camera and annoyed people into giving him a fling as a picture-taker himself although he was and is completely self-tutored. Whatever the Sneads and the Settles were doing, the boy Comegys absorbed. "I just sort of picked it up," he says. He remains a non-technician who is instinctively great—"I'm as basic as you can get."

They grudgingly hired him as a staff member on a probationary basis. If a star wasn't born then, a budding one was tolerated.

Fred confesses he couldn't make it as a walk-on in these times. He perhaps would walk into a newspaper building, but that would be it. They are hiring college graduates, journalism school people. But I love his answer to that: "I don't know that a college degree is necessary to take good pictures."

A remarkable angle to this book and Comegys' national championship portfolio is that all the photos were taken within a 50-mile-radius of exotic downtown Wilmington. (Just think of all the legwork he could have saved, had a 50-mile-range zoom been invented.) So who says nothing happens in Wilmington? To Comegys and his incredible eye, he couldn't have a more fertile field. Contrast his collection to the other Photographer-of-the-Year winners. The magazine honor went to a National Geographic fellow who took pictures of trains in India. Best Photo Essay OTY was won by a Boston Globe man. The subject was starvation in Ethiopia.

Comegys and friend

Comegys needs no trips on jet planes to find subjects to study and with which to excel. A trip to the ball park in Philadelphia or the seashore in Rehoboth Beach is about the budget range for the department. In between, Fred's magic touch catches cloistered nuns, the work behind Italian festivals, kids on playgrounds, height pictures from bridges and buildings that give the readers vertigo, river traffic, triple-A college football. He loves it. "This," he says, "is my scene. I care about what my so-called local pictures look like, because taking pictures is all I do. I like to find the extraordinary in the ordinary."

One spring they did assign him to the Phillies' camp in Clearwater, Fla. He must have thought he required a passport. Once he arrived and conquered the culture shock, he routinely went around taking pictures that had to be a sports department's delight. That was the year he also got his name on the Philadelphia sports pages. This training afternoon, Fred had his back to the outfield, focusing a scene. Boom! Joe Hoerner, one of the Phillies pitchers engaging in a drill in which they were shagging thrown fly balls, ran smack into the photographer from Wilmington. Hoerner and his prized left arm went down in a heap. No damage done, however—but it was a scare. Fred went on to have a much better year than Hoerner.

Almost without fail, I can look at a picture in the paper and know immediately that it is one of his, without squintingly checking the credit line. At the risk of sounding like an art critic, my reaction is that his best are to be savored, absorbed. There is a crispness to them; whatever he does to determine how to calculate the lighting, he gets marvelous results. Black and white becomes beautiful.

And, of course, I am not alone in my amateur respect for the Comegys touch. I once did an interview with Teresa Wright, the actress, who was appearing at the Playhouse. Fred was assigned to do the art. We talked in the Hotel du Pont's Brandywine Room and Fred showed up later on cue. He suggested that Miss Wright might want to have the photo taken outdoors, across the street, against a Rodney Square balustrade.

A couple of weeks later, I received a letter from the actress. She appreciated all the paper had done for her, she wrote—"and such a remarkable photograph! My husband cannot get over how your man made such great use of back-lighting."

You ask a fellow pro what makes this guy what he is. "He has a feel for composition," says Pat Crowe, "and he has the ability to capture a moment on film. His style is simple, clean, graphic." I will drink to that.

So why does he keep hanging his knitted hat in minor-league Wilmington? A natural question. New York, Washington, Philadephia, you know he could make it there, and anywhere. He admits he has had offers. "But I'm afraid of the big cities, and also just plain lazy. I've always been a home boy."

This is a little frightening, but Comegys was the oldest person ever to win it in the 42-year-old Photographer of the Year contest—and he was all of 44. Fred thinks they were a bit surprised he wasn't burned out at his age.

Comegys class

I am pleased to report that Fred Comegys is not quite ready for a halo fitting. He, after all, remains one of us mortals. Although he is humble in victory, his temper level fits right into the Ego City that is a newspaper office. He can groan with the best when they slip him what he thinks—and undoubtedly is—a poor assignment. And he will also say a few words when he thinks his picture is badly cropped, badly played or, zounds, even pushed aside. Nobody's perfect, even a perfectionist. But he has earned this right. He works hard. He is one of the aces at his trade. Any more, I couldn't stand.

Turn the pages. You will find you will be doing it very slowly. You will be looking through Comegys' lens.

PEOPLE...

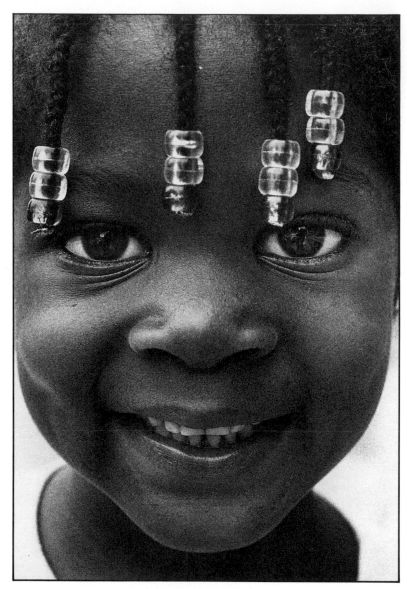

Laquesta Dukes, Wilmington, 1980

John Sweetman, 86, awaits his daily paper outside of Newark, May 1984

Hay-on-Wye, Wales, 1983

Steve Mikulcik with his new puppy, Old Baltimore Pike near Newark, Fall 1987

Wilbur Easter, 71, near his Townsend home, 1972

Joe Frazier, Philadephia, Summer 1973

*Rev. Jesse Jackson at Lincoln University,
Oxford, Pa., June 1969*

Muhammad Ali, Deer Lake Training Camp, 1974

Jackie Robinson, Hotel DuPont, Feb. 1968

Big
Nose
Sammy

Big Nose Sammy, 1973

Lyndon B. Johnson at 9th and Market Street, Wilmington,
Oct. 1966

Hubert Humphrey visits Wilmington to commemorate
Memorial Bridge twin spans, Sept. 1968

Ingrid Bergman, Wilmington, March 1972

I.M. Pei at 12th and Market Street, Oct. 1970

Sister Mary Francis tosses a football during recreation period, Visitation Sisters of St. Francis de Sales, Wilmington, 1984.

Pete DuPont, Campaign of March 1978

Joe Biden officially announced candidacy for President of the United States of America, June 1987, Radisson Hotel

Santa's Easy Riders, Toys for Tots, 1978

Ted, April, Tajuana, and Monica Gray walking across wet grass, Wilmington, Spring 1979

Herbie

Pilgrim and Pals *Walter Spencer, Eric Lloyd, Megan Isaacson at Forwood Elementary School, November 1985*

Fran Swift and Blue at Gordy Estates attract a friendly crowd, Summer 1983

Dinner for 2000 *Columbia Alsia, 80, St. Anthony's Italian Festival, Wilmington, 1985*

Hairy Ride *John Kmetz, Newark resident enjoys the James E. Strates Show, Prices Corner, May 1987*

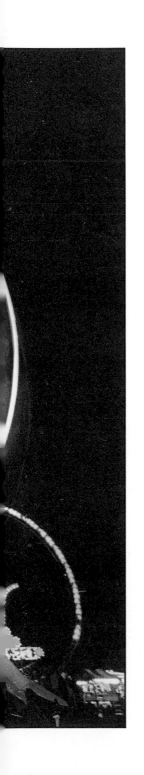

Happy Halloween *George Breeding and Eric Ferguson, 1981*

Under The Hot Sun *Strawberry fields, Ocean View, 1972*

The Guitar Man on Second Street, Wilmington, Aug. 1973

Ron Klopher and Izsak the Komondor, Wilmington
Kennel Club Show, 1981

*Andrew Schreiner "cooling off", Rockford Tower
Condominiums, Summer 1986*

Nobel Peace prize winner *Elie Wiesel, Wilmington,*
Sept. 1987

Noble Winners

Charles J. Pedersen, Salem, New Jersey, December 1987

Candace and Hershey, Banning Park, 1984

Tubby Raymond

Tubby wins *Victory over Colgate, Sept. 1978*

Tubby loses *20 game streak ends, 1973*

*Governor Michael N. Castle Hotel DuPont, speech on
prison system, 1987*

General William Westmoreland speaks to Vietnam War Veterans, Sept. 1983

Daniel Frawley, March 1978 in rugby game

U.S. Senator Edward Kennedy at St. Marks, 1972

Carol Ashcock circus worker for 57 years, May 1972

Mary Scales Day at 100th birthday. She was a U.S. Army nurse during World War I, Nov. 1987

Charles Parks in his studio, 1985

Old man at parade on Market Street, 1970

Muddy

A Moment of Reflection *Mrs. Florence R. Crumlish, 1972*

Old Wood Lover *retired carpenter J. Morton McCardell,*
82, of Rising Sun, Maryland, 1985

Tetu Robinson walks her pet Iguana, Wilmington, Summer 1970

PLACES...

The last ride of the season *Lenape Park, Sept. 1971*

All that remains *300-year-old Episcopal Church in New Castle, Feb. 1980*

After the rain, two Huck Finns ride a styrofoam raft,
New Castle, 1984

Coast Guard's Eagle rides up Delaware River, June 1982

QE2 on the Delaware River. She makes a stop at Edgemoor on her way to Philadelphia, April 1982

Manhattan arrives, New York City, 1969

Letting it all hang out *Billy Reardon Jr. and Sr.,
Delaware Bay near Lewes, Summer 1985*

Manning the Sails *Welcoming salute to the city of Philadelphia 300th birthday, Penns Landing, June 1982*

Little Emma Jean Swartzentruber sweeps the steps of an Amish schoolhouse outside Dover, 1985

Quarters from Heaven *Armored car dumped $4000*
worth of quarters on Concord Pike, 1983

On a roll *Brandywine High School principal Larry Hobdell on first day of school, Sept. 1986*

Eugene West, scrubbrush in hand, rides high as he gives
Ceasar Rodney a washdown, March 1971

Down the stretch, Delaware Park, 1978

*Harry Heller and his crew clean the Delaware Memorial
Bridge, 1976*

View from Harlech Castle, Wales, 1983

Punkers, Dublin Ireland, 1985

Beating the heat *Hoopes Reservoir, Summer 1973*

Rear View *Market Street Bridge, Wilmington, 1968*

The hands of Sister Mary Sulpice, age 92

Sister Margaret Mary and Mother Superior Mary Raphaelle walk in the cemetery at the monastery, Wilmington, 1984

The Pole Position *Amish Farmer Jacob Mast takes back seat on ''logging wheels'' while his son helps upfront, near Dover, 1985*

Spiderweb *St. Georges Bridge, Oct. 1971*

Tractor tracks, May 1969 on a farm near Dover

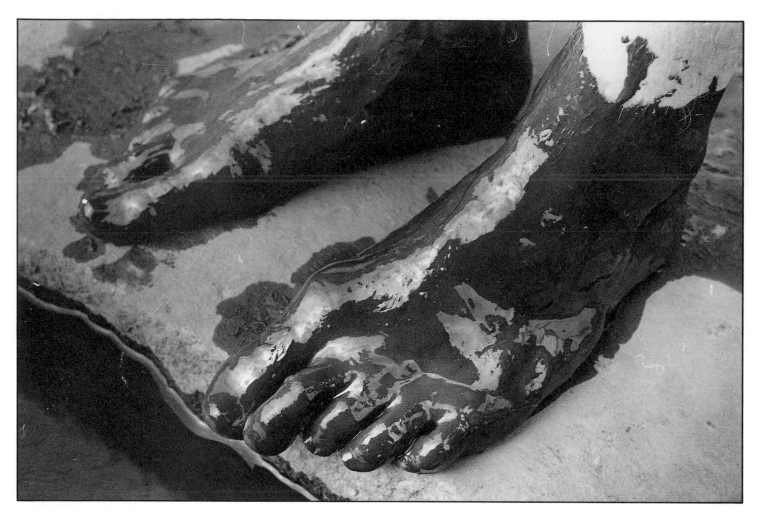

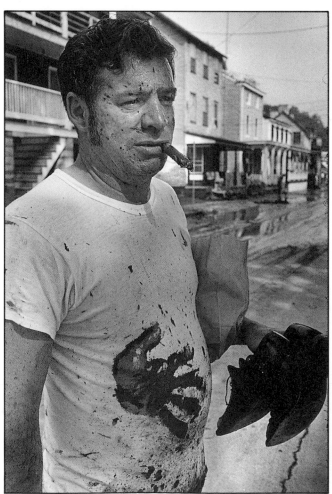

Mud covers all *Port Deposit, June 26, 1972*

Port Deposit Flood

The lion's share of fun *McCullough Elementary School,*
Garfield Park, New Castle, 1985

A Phanatic Chase *Manny Sanguillen of Pittsburg Pirates and Davey Raymond, Veterans Stadium, 1978*

Brandywine
River

Baptism in Brandywine *July 1971*

In the Drink *Scott Alvanos and his horse, Scout, Brandywine River, Summer 1985*

Summer swim in Brandywine *June 1981*

Easy Rider *Pennsville, New Jersey, July 1970*   100

Owl *Tri State Bird Rescue*

The Blizzard of '78, Wilmington

Basket for a Bonnet *Elsmere*

Flipped Out at Rehoboth Beach *Rick Marshall, Summer 1986*

Steel Patterns *Bear 1969*

Balcony Seats *Mike Caffery and Jim Cyphers on 18th floor of the new Bank of Delaware Building, March 1986*

Rear View on a country road *Stratsburg, Pa., Aug. 1980*

Amish tobacco harvest *Lancaster, Pa., 1984*

The Drive In *Marie Bassill and Pat Hurley, Naamans Drive In, July 1982*

Clean Block Campaign *Wilmington, Sept. 1968*

Slum Silhouette *Wilmington, April 1972*

EVENTS...

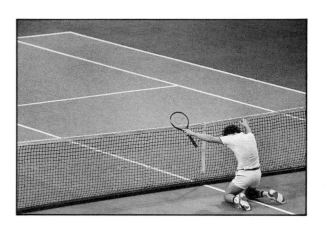

The Great Wallenda walks above Veterans Stadium
Aug. 14, 1972

All is cool!

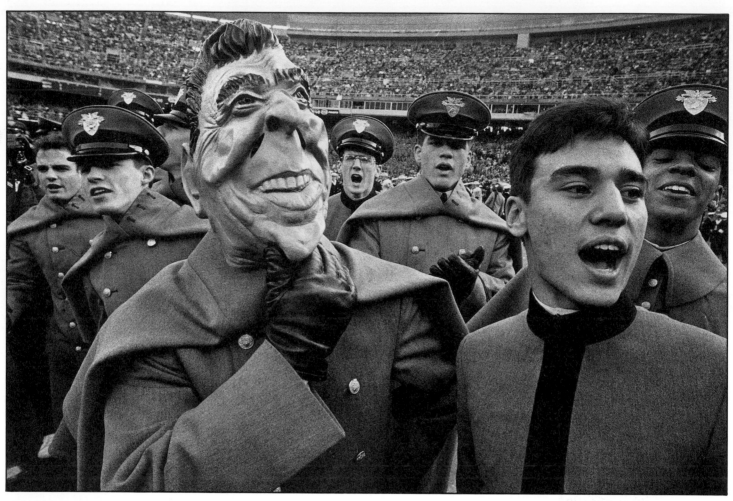

Presidential Partiality *A familiar face in the crowd,*
Army Navy Game, Veterans Stadium, 1985

Double Take *Delaware Navy Football, 1986*

Midshipman, Army Navy Game, 1985

McEnroe humbled *losing to Mayotte, Philadelphia, Feb. 1987*

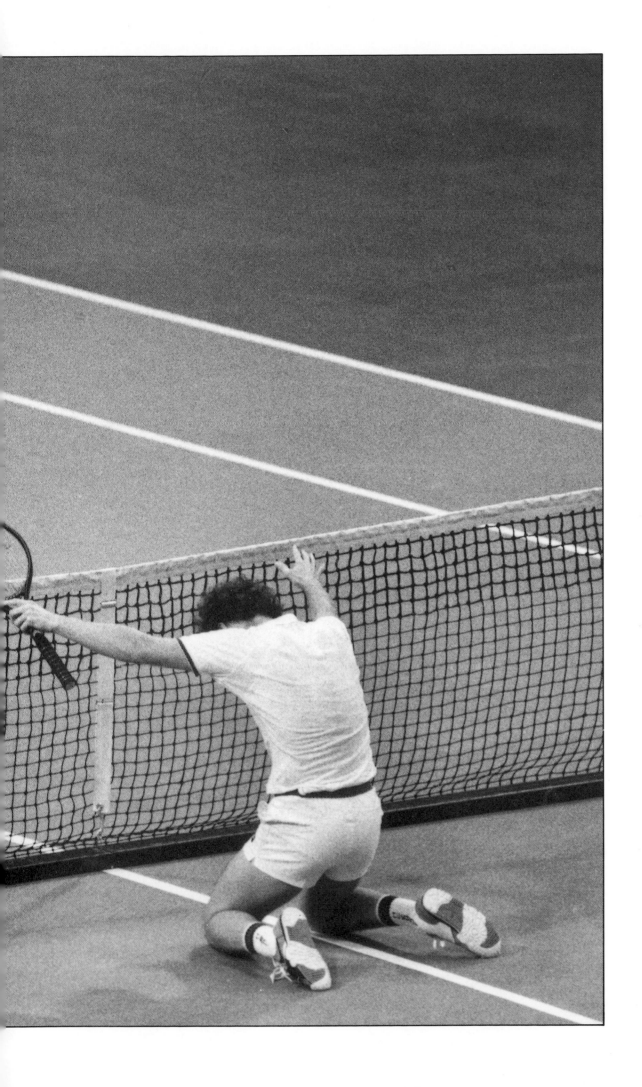

Wheelchair Olympics *University of Delaware, April 1983*

Phillies in Series! *Mike Schmidt and Al Holland, Oct. 1983*

Doc's Final House Call

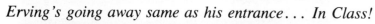

Erving's going away same as his entrance... In Class!

Fallen Marines back from Beirut, Oct. 1983

Marine Comes Home *Tom Little and Son, Oct. 1983*

Something to Cry About *Blue Hens defeat Villanova, Oct. 1971*

Concord, Hares Corner, Nov. 1987

Tom Fede keeps watch over Goodyear Blimp, Wilmington Airport, 1984

Winged Memories *Harold Gregg, former pilot, stares at the Texas Raider a B-17G, Wilmington Airport, Aug. 1986*

JKF Stadium Inside-Outside

Fairhill Races

They're off!, Spring 1978

Down and Dirty

Figures it's safe . . .

Safe at last!

Newark snaps Middletown's 53-game winning streak, 1967

Thrill of Victory *Brandywiner's Alison Rheingold,
Diana Despiaumolina, Becky Bundens, Allison Hoen and
Heather Gonser, 1987*

Great Peace March 1986

A Fond Thank You *Heather McQuown meets John G. Leach on his 83rd birthday, Oct. 1984*

137

1986 Riots

Our Lady of Peace, Rodney Square, 1982

Face for the Fourth *Michelle Bloothoofd, Rockwood Museum, July 4th, 1982*

Pagan Funeral, Corpus Christi Church, Elsmere, 1984

Ku Klux Klan rally, Bear 1965

Robert Pitcairn helps passenger across his back,
Oct. 1975

Campaign Fodder, Delaware City, 1968

*15th Annual Delaware All Star High School Football
Game, Summer 1970*

Close Shave *Salvador Santiago from Puerto Rico plays baseball with Wilmington Little Leaguers*

Delicate Dream *Barbie Andrejewski, National Gymnastics Championships at University of Delaware Field House, June 1987*

Cape May - Lewes Ferry, 1987

King Carl XVI Gustaf and Queen Silvia arrive at Fort Christina Park during re-enactment of 1638 landing, April 1988

ENTERTAINMENT...

Born in the U.S.A. *Bruce Springsteen, Spectrum, 1985*

Purple Rain *Prince, Spectrum, Nov. 1984*

Dallas Green from Newport, Delaware is manager of
Philadelphia Phillies Pennant Winners, 1980

lies

Miss Gloria Swanson *"Women's Lib is Nonsense", Hotel*
DuPont, 1971

For Maximum Workout *Shirley Wintren strains with weights, Wilmington, July 1984*

Having fun at picnic in Wilmington, 1970...

Pete Rose

Diving into 3rd *Veterans Stadium, Philadelphia, Summer 1981*

Joe Cocker, Spectrum, 1972

Alice Cooper, Playhouse, 1971

Kiss In Action, Philadelphia, 1978

Cool Cat... Gunther Geble Williams

Circus *Prices Corner, 1973*

Robert Cline, "The Elephant Keeper"

Live Aid
Summer 1985

A concertgoer shows his colors

Bill Bergey in Action *Veterans Stadium, Oct. 1975*

Bill Bergey

Dodo Cheyney, Wilmington Country Club, 1982

Out on a Limb *Missy Meharg, University of Delaware, 1984*

Satchel Paige, Veterans Stadium, Philadelphia

Tex Ritter, Wilmington, 1973

Arnold Palmer, Senior PGA Tournament

The Juice *O.J. Simpson, 1971*

Billy Cunningham, Dave DeBusschere, 1971

Old Pros

Chester born, Danny Murtaugh became manager Pittsburgh Pirates, 1971

Victory! *Mike Outten, B.J. Dryden, Delmar Senior League, 1984*

Faked Out! *State Tournament, March 1969*

In Position *Malone and Jabar, Spectrum, Philadelphia, 1985*

The Music and the Sparkle *Michael Jackson, JFK Stadium, Sept. 1984*

Count Basie, University of Delaware, March 1969

Pro Pyramid *Celtics and Sixers, Spectrum, 1983*

Glenn Wilson shatters bat, Veterans Stadium,
Philadelphia, 1986

Annual Turkey Bowl

*An annual football game in Wilmington, 1984 . . .
a little bit of fun in the mud!*

A Message From The News-Journal

Fred Comegys came to work for the News-Journal Company in 1959, when he was 18. It has been his working home ever since. When he began, the company was already a Delaware institution. Today, Fred Comegys is a Delaware institution as well.

He didn't begin by taking pictures. He started in the engraving department, working with machines that turned other people's pictures into the etched impressions needed to print them in the newspaper. A few years later, he began working in the photography department as a lab technician. Finally, at the age of 24, he earned the title of staff photographer.

There are nearly as many definitions for staff photographer as there are individuals who hold the title. In the case of Fred Comegys, the title is incomplete without the modifier, prize-winning. That accurately reflects his success in scores of competitions over the years. It has been particularly appropriate since 1985, when he was named National Newspaper Photographer of the Year.

On his worst days, Fred Comegys is a competent photographer. At his best, as is obvious in the pages of this book, he is an artist. Those of us who have worked closely with him over the years respected the first and learned to live with the second. Fred Comegys is no more temperamental than many other truly creative individuals, but no less so, either. Woe to the editor who reproduced one of his masterpieces in less than the billboard display he thought it deserved. And heaven help those who wantonly destroyed carefully composed Comegys photographs by cropping them ''to fit.''

Readers of these pages will quickly recognize that Fred Comegys has an inner eye that sees things we ordinary beings do not. His instinct for patterns, his pursuit of a different perspective, his sense of when to experiment, his appreciation of people, their faces and costumes; all are the ingredients in his recipe for superb craftsmanship.

This volume is not a valedictory. Fred Comegys is still a young man, from whom readers of the News-Journal papers can continue to anticipate the kind of photographs they have come to treasure. As for those of us who have come to think of The News-Journal Company as our second family, Fred Comegys is a favorite son.

J. Donald Brandt
Editor
The News-Journal Company

Philly Phanatic and Fred Comegys

"Someone should have made a book on Fred's photography years ago."

This book was made possible by The News-Journal Company, Pat Crowe, Sal DeVivo, J. Donald Brandt, Al Cartwright, Ted Paul, and most importantly, Fred Comegys.

A. Amira and J. Jared

The Jared Company